WEST CHICAGO PUBLIC LIBRARY DISTRICT

3 66 8 00105 1295

P9-CFI-868

AC 2-7622 10/00

ANIMAL TRACKERS

IN WOODS
&
FORESTS

Tessa Paul

CRABTREE
Publishing Company

West Chicago Public Library District
118 West Washington
West Chicago, IL 60185-2803
Phone # (630) 231-1552

CRABTREE
Publishing Company

350 Fifth Avenue	360 York Road, R.R.4	73 Lime Walk
Suite 3308	Niagara-on-the-Lake	Headington, Oxford
New York, NY 10118	Ontario L0S 1J0	England OX3 7AD

Editor **Bobbie Kalman**
Assistant Editor **Virginia Mainprize**
Designers **Emma Humphreys-Davies Richard Shiner Melissa Stokes**

Illustrations by
Front cover: Robin Bouttell/WLAA; Introduction: Robin Bouttell/WLAA, Rosalind Hewitt, Rod Sutterby, BarbaraWalker;
Robin Bouttell/WLAA, (p.10 – 11), Graham Allan/Linden Artists (p.7), Mike Atkinson (p.28 – 29), Robin Bouttell/WLAA (p.10 – 11),
Robin Budden/WLAA (p.14 – 15), Jim Channell (p.18 – 19, 20 – 21), Niel Cox/WLAA (p.6), Brian Edwards/WLAA (p.16 – 17),
Rosalind Hewitt (p.12), Terence Lambert (p.26 – 27), Mick Loates/Linden Artists, (p.30 – 31), John Morris/WLAA (p.8 – 9), Colin Newman
(p.28), Denys Ovenden (p.22 – 23), Chris Rose (p.26 – 27), Valérie Stetton (p.12 – 13), Rod Sutterby (p.23, 29, 30),
Kim Thompson (p.24 – 25),

First printed 1997
Copyright © 1997 Marshall Cavendish Ltd.

All rights reserved. No part of this publication may be reproduced in any form or by any means – graphic, electronic or mechanical, including photocopying,
recording, taping or information storage and retrieval systems – without the prior written permission of the publishers and the copyright holder.

Cataloging-in-Publication Data

Paul, Tessa
In woods and forests / Tessa Paul
p. cm. – – (Animal Trackers)
Includes index.
Summary: Explains how to track ten common forest animals, including the opossum, raccoon, and red squirrel.
ISBN 0-86505-584-X – – ISBN 0-86505-592-0 (pbk.)
1. Forest animals – – Juvenile literature.
2. Animal tracks – Juvenile literature. [1. Forest animals. 2. Animal tracks.]
I. Title.   II. Series: Paul, Tessa . Animal trackers .
QL112.P37 1997   591.73 – –dc21   96-39672   CIP AC

Printed and bound in Malaysia

CONTENTS

INTRODUCTION

The forest is home to many animals. There they find their food, eating leaves and berries or hunting other animals. In the branches of the trees, squirrels jump and swing. Birds make their nests. Martens hunt for eggs. Under the ground, animals dig tunnels, making dens for themselves and nests for their babies.

Some woodland animals have moved out of the forest into towns and cities. Sometimes, they eat the food people have thrown away. Sometimes, they live in barns, chimneys, and under houses.

Wherever animals go, they leave signs. They may be tooth or claw marks on a tree, bumps under the snow, or paw prints in the earth. They show the places where animals live, eat, or sleep.

This book shows you how to find these animal signs in the forest and in the city. You will learn how to spot a badger's home or a magpie's nest. You will find out which animals come out during the day or hunt at night. Soon, you will become an animal detective.

OPOSSUM

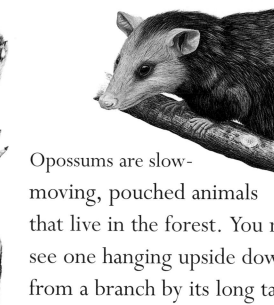

Opossums are slow-moving, pouched animals that live in the forest. You might see one hanging upside down from a branch by its long tail. Because opossums have a strong smell, most other animals keep away from them.

OPOSSUM FOOD
Opossums will eat just about anything. They eat fruit, berries, insects, and small animals such as mice and voles. They love eggs, and sometimes they will steal them from birds' nests and chicken coops.

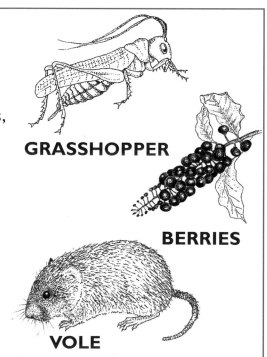

GRASSHOPPER

BERRIES

VOLE

LIVING SPACE
Opossums eat at night. During the day, they rest in trees or hollow logs.

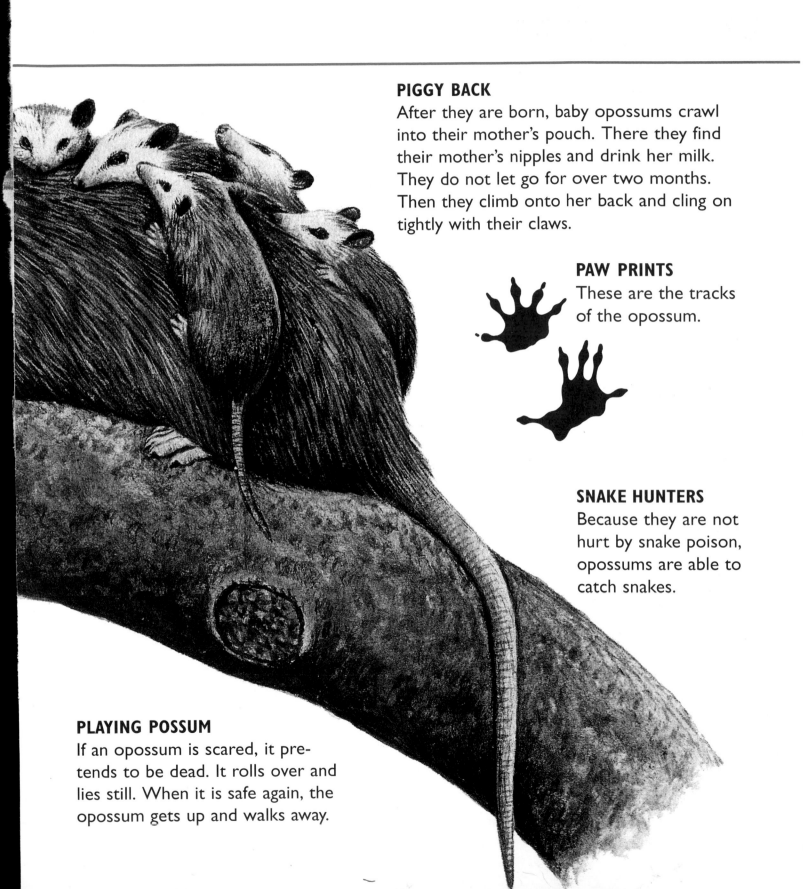

PIGGY BACK

After they are born, baby opossums crawl into their mother's pouch. There they find their mother's nipples and drink her milk. They do not let go for over two months. Then they climb onto her back and cling on tightly with their claws.

PAW PRINTS

These are the tracks of the opossum.

SNAKE HUNTERS

Because they are not hurt by snake poison, opossums are able to catch snakes.

PLAYING POSSUM

If an opossum is scared, it pretends to be dead. It rolls over and lies still. When it is safe again, the opossum gets up and walks away.

RACCOON

Raccoons are smart. They know how to use their hands to catch food, or even open a jar. They make their dens in dark places. They like to live near rivers and streams.

NIGHT SCHOOL

Raccoons come out at night. When the sun goes down, the mother and her babies, called kits, search for food.

FRESH FISH

Fish bones near a river might mean raccoons ate there. They use their front paws to catch fish. They also eat berries, insects, small animals, and birds' eggs. Raccoons like to wash their food before eating it.

HOWLS AND HISSES
Raccoons are noisy. They purr, hiss, and growl. They make a noise like the hooting of an owl. When caught, they give a high, sad cry.

SHARP CLAWS
The tracks show the paw and the sharp, strong claws.

Some raccoons never live in a forest. They spend all their lives in towns and cities near people. Raccoons love roof tops and chimneys. Sometimes, they will live in attics or drain pipes.

CITY SOUNDS
At night, you may hear the clatter of a garbage can. The raccoons are looking for their dinner.

CLEAN CREATURES
Raccoons like to wash their food. They will use a birdbath or a fishpond if there is no other water.

SWEET BUT STRONG
Raccoons are gentle animals. But if they are cornered, they will fight bravely.

PORCUPINE

Porcupines live alone. They come out at night to look for food. In the day, they rest in trees, hidden among the leaves. They are good swimmers and will cross a lake looking for water lilies.

NOT CLEAR
Only part of the paws shows in the tracks.

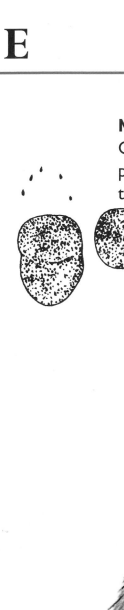

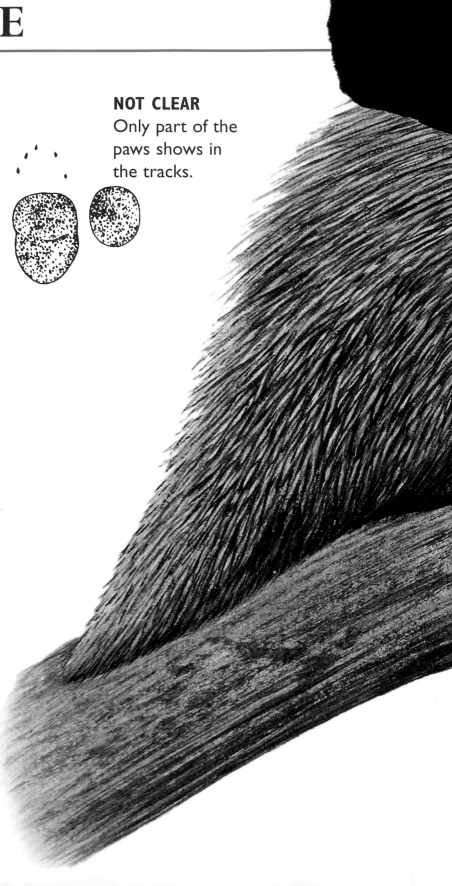

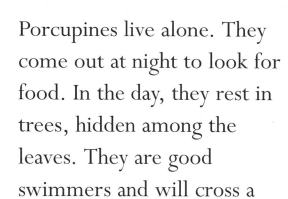

EATING TREES
Under the bark of a tree there is a moist, sweet layer of sap. You can see where a porcupine has stripped the bark for this food.

MUSICAL NOTES

Some people say that porcupines sing 'doh-ray-me.' They also whistle, grunt, and loudly chatter their teeth.

HOME PATHS

Porcupines move slowly and do not roam far from home. They use the same trails to and from their dens. In the winter, they plough paths under the snow.

SHARP DEFENSE

The hairs on the back, head, and tail of a porcupine are like sharp needles. They are called quills. When a porcupine is attacked, it turns around and swings its tail at the enemy. Animals that attack porcupines often get a mouthful of quills.

MAGPIE

Magpies are large, noisy birds. Their tail feathers are as long as their bodies. This makes them easy to spot. They have loud voices, and they chatter, scold, and whistle. In late winter, groups of magpies gather in tree tops and chase, fight, and play with each other.

FANNED FLIGHT
The long tail feathers spread out when the bird flies. The central feathers are extra long.

LARGE DOMES
The large nests are made of twigs and mud. They are lined with grass and covered with sticks. Entrances are on the side. Magpies lay six to eight speckled eggs.

SHARP BEAKS
Magpies will land on a cow and peck the insects off it. This helps the cow but often leaves sores on its skin.

FAVORITE FOODS

Magpies eat animals that are already dead. They also eat grain, fruit, berries, and insects. Other birds are scared of them because magpies often steal their eggs and eat the baby birds.

UNEVEN
The toe is slightly off center.

RED SQUIRREL

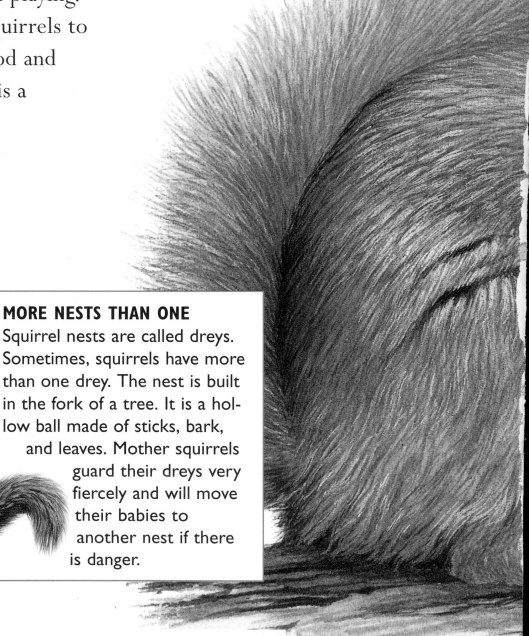

Red squirrels like pine forests, but they also live in leafy trees. They seem to play together, jumping from branch to branch and chasing each other on the ground. But they are not playing. They are telling other squirrels to keep away from their food and den. Their loud chatter is a warning sign.

MORE NESTS THAN ONE

Squirrel nests are called dreys. Sometimes, squirrels have more than one drey. The nest is built in the fork of a tree. It is a hollow ball made of sticks, bark, and leaves. Mother squirrels guard their dreys very fiercely and will move their babies to another nest if there is danger.

SIGN POSTS

It is not difficult to track squirrels. They have favorite places where they eat, usually a stump or log. Squirrels tear up pine cones, leaving the stems uneaten. Leftover pine stems can build up into huge piles.

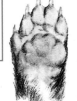

TOOTH MARKS

IIn the spring, squirrels tear off the bark from maple branches to suck up the sweet sap. Look for bite spots on roots or chewed bark to see if a squirrel lives nearby.

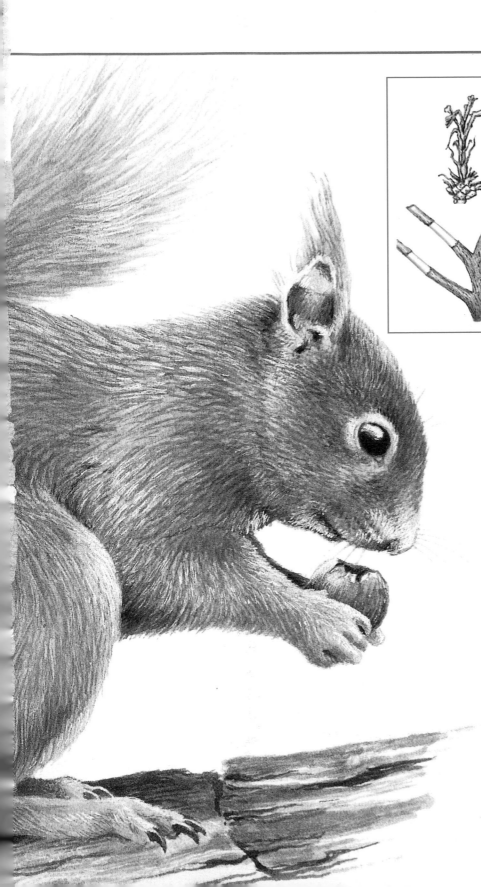

SOFT PAWS

Unless the earth is soft or muddy, squirrel tracks are hard to see.

WINTER PANTRY

Squirrels bury their food in the ground or store it in piles called caches. In winter, squirrels build tunnels under the snow from one cache to another.

BADGER

Badgers live in an underground home called a sett. It has long, deep tunnels that lead to sleeping areas.

COSY NESTS
Mother badger builds a nest at the end of one of the tunnels. She lines it with dry grass for her babies.

STEAM SHOVEL CLAWS
Badgers are strong diggers with short, stout legs and feet with long, thick claws.

PIT STOPS
Badgers have places where they rest with their food before returning home to their sett. A dent in a field or a hollow under a bush may mean that a badger has been there.

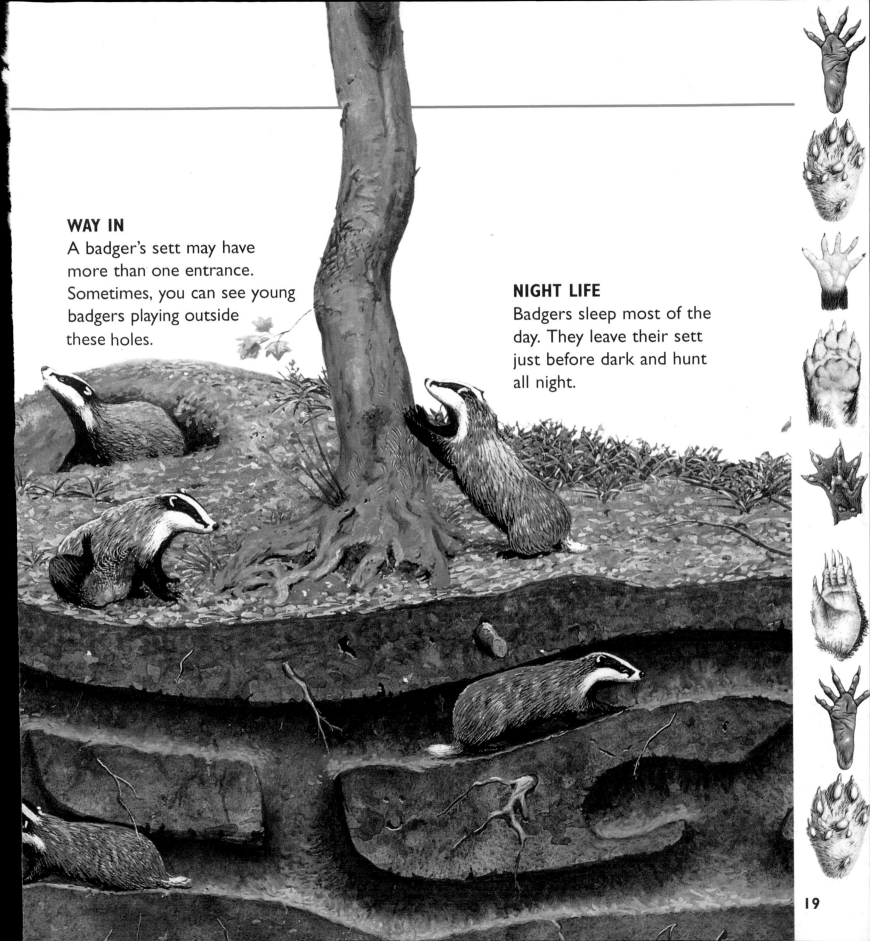

WAY IN
A badger's sett may have more than one entrance. Sometimes, you can see young badgers playing outside these holes.

NIGHT LIFE
Badgers sleep most of the day. They leave their sett just before dark and hunt all night.

19

Badgers eat rabbits, field mice, and small birds. They love honey and will eat the whole nest, bees and all. Sometimes, if a badger catches a big rabbit, it will store it in an old den and go back later to eat it. Badgers bark at other badgers who try to take their food. They also bark to warn of danger. The babies make squeaking noises.

A CLEAR SHOW
The tracks are heavy and easy to see.

COOLING OFF
In summer, badgers may cool themselves by squatting in the water. They even swim and catch fish.

HOME ROUTE
Badgers use the same trails when they leave or return to their setts.

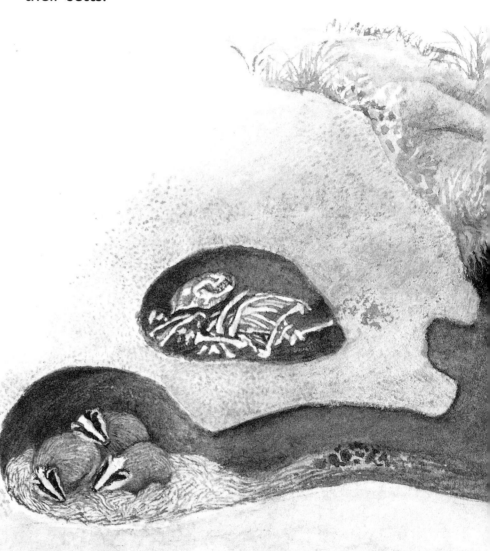

BITS AND PIECES
Outside the entrance to the sett, you will see a mound of earth which piles up as the badger digs its tunnels. There you may find bits of bone and fur from animals the badger has eaten.

SCRATCH MARKS
Badgers sharpen and clean their claws by scratching on trees.

21

SKUNK

Skunks are quiet animals that search for food at night. They live in dens in the ground. They eat bees, snakes, grubs, and worms. They love birds' eggs and may raid a farmer's chicken coop.

FAMILY LIFE

Just before dark, the mother skunk and her young leave the den. They go looking for food. In the winter, they hibernate with other skunk families in underground dens. There they build warm nests of dried grass and leaves.

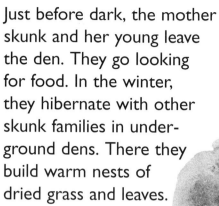

PAWS
Skunks are excellent diggers. Their front feet have five long, curved claws.

KEEP AWAY
When in danger, a skunk does not fight or struggle. It turns its back on its attacker, raises its tail, and stamps its front feet as a warning. Then, it sprays a stinking mist into the animal's face. Few animals risk going near the smelly skunk.

BAT

Bats sleep during the day and come out at dusk. Bats fly fast but never bump into things. They make shrill squeaks which bounce back like an echo when they hit something. This tells the bat how close it is to a tree, a building, or even a small flying insect.

NOT BIRDS

Bats are not birds, they are mammals. They are furry animals that nurse their babies with mother's milk.

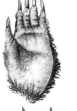

FLIGHT REFRESHMENT

Bats are graceful fliers. They glide over the surface of a pond or river, dip their heads down, and sip up the water without stopping.

BAT COLONY
Hundreds of mother bats live together in caves, barns, or the attics of houses. There they sleep and nurse their young. They hang upside down when they sleep. At night, the mothers leave their babies in the bat nursery and go hunting for food.

ACROBATS OF THE AIR
Bats hunt while flying. They can swerve, swoop, and turn tight corners in the air. They catch moths, mosquitos, and other insects.

CHIPMUNK

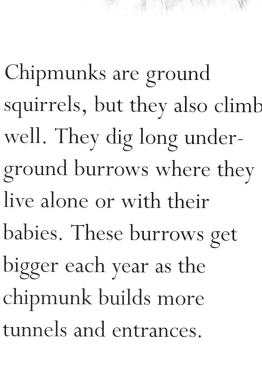

MENU PLANNING

Chipmunks stuff nuts, pine cones, and small insects into their mouth until their cheeks bulge. Then, they run to their burrows and store the food for winter.

Chipmunks are ground squirrels, but they also climb well. They dig long underground burrows where they live alone or with their babies. These burrows get bigger each year as the chipmunk builds more tunnels and entrances.

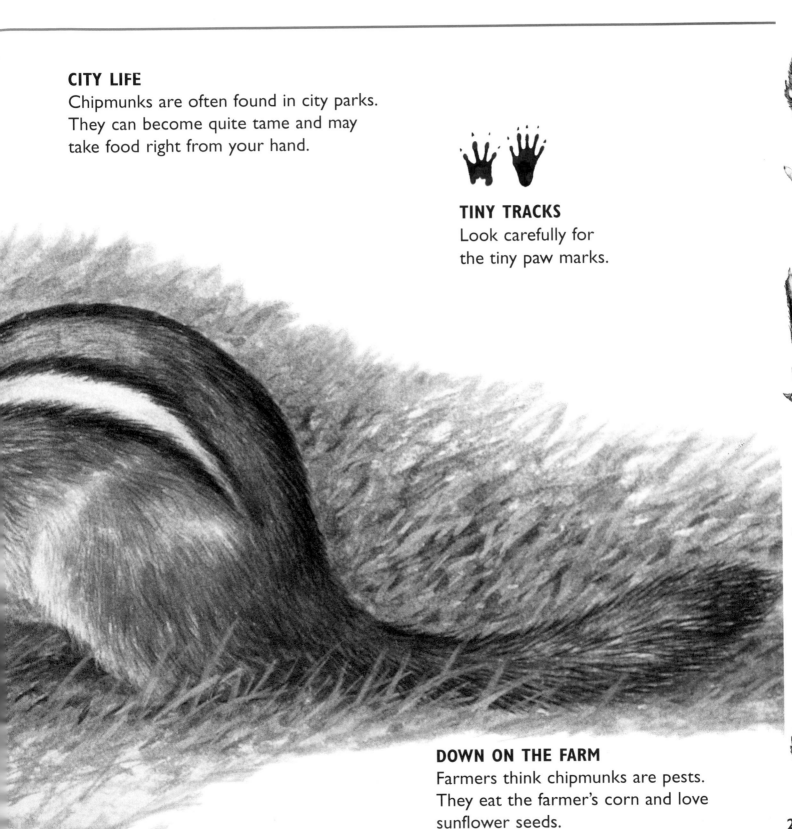

CITY LIFE
Chipmunks are often found in city parks.
They can become quite tame and may
take food right from your hand.

TINY TRACKS
Look carefully for
the tiny paw marks.

DOWN ON THE FARM
Farmers think chipmunks are pests.
They eat the farmer's corn and love
sunflower seeds.

WEASEL

The fur of the weasel is the same color as dry leaves and shadows. In the winter, the fur of some weasels becomes as white as snow. When an animal's fur matches the places where it lives, we say the animal is camouflaged. The weasel is so well camouflaged that it is difficult to see.

PAW PRINTS
A weasel's prints are easy to see in fresh snow.

WELL SHAPED
Their long, thin body make weasels excellent hunters. They can U-turn, somersault, and wiggle through tiny spaces. They can chase a rabbit right down its hole.

A FLASH OF FUR

A weasel can move very fast. It hides in cracks between rocks, then zooms out to pounce on its prey.

VICIOUS HUNTERS

Because they have such good hearing, sight, and smell, weasels are wonderful trackers. They often attack animals much larger than themselves.

TAKE-OVERS

Weasels do not build their own dens. They move into mole tunnels or rabbit burrows. There they build a nest of dried leaves and grasses. They line it with the fur and feathers of animals they have eaten.

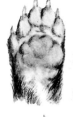

MARTEN

With their sharp claws and thin body, martens are excellent hunters. Most of their hunting is on the ground. They also climb trees and dive down onto their prey. They use their long, bushy tail for balance when leaping across branches. In winter, they tunnel under snow looking for food.

STRONG MARKS
Martens make heavy tracks that are easy to see.

NESTING PLACES
In early spring, a mother marten can have three or four babies. She raises them in a nest of grass under rocks or in a hollow tree.

ON THE HUNT

Martens hunt squirrels. To escape, the squirrel must run to a branch that is too thin for the marten.

HARD TO SEE

Since martens hunt mainly at night and in forests, they are seldom seen by people.

AN EXCELLENT MOUSER

Martens hunt mice and squirrels. They dig up insect nests, attack nesting birds, and eat their eggs. When hunting is good, martens bury their extra food.

31

INDEX

GLOSSARY

Burrow - The tunnel or hole in the ground dug by an animal for its home.

Camouflage - Many animals blend with the color of the place where they live. This is called camouflage. Camouflage protects an animal from its enemies and hides it when it is trying to catch other animals.

Colony - A large group of animals of the same kind living together is called a colony. They build their dens or nests in one shared place.

Den - The home or hiding place of a wild animal.

Drey - A squirrel's nest is called a drey.

Hibernate - Animals that hibernate spend the winter in a deep sleep.

Mammal - An animal that does not lay eggs but gives birth to its young. It also feeds its babies with milk from its breast.

Prey - An animal that is hunted by another animal is called the prey.

Sett - A badger's underground den and tunnels are called a sett.